DOMESTIC SLAVERY

IN ITS

RELATIONS WITH WEALTH

AN ORATION

PRONOUNCED IN THE

Cuban Democratic Athenaeum of New York.

ON THE EVENING OF THE 1st OF JANUARY, 1854.

BY DON LORENZO ALLO,

PROFESSOR OF POLITICAL ECONOMY.

Having had the pleasure of publishing this little work in Spanish, for the purpose of free circulation in Cuba, I now present it to my American friends, in their own language, dedicating the translation to my worthy and lamented friend, whose last effort it was.

DOMINGO DE GOICOURIA.

New York, January 1, 1855.

NEW YORK:

W. H. TINSON, PRINTER AND STEREOTYPER, 24 BEEKMAN ST.

1855.

DOMESTIC SLAVERY

IN ITS

RELATIONS WITH WEALTH.

GENTLEMEN:—

I propose to treat, this evening, of Domestic Slavery in its relations with wealth; and I deem it convenient to divide the subject into three parts, of which the following are the mottoes: *First.* Slavery is antagonistic to wealth. *Second.* Refutation of the arguments in support of slavery. *Third.* The means of abolishing slavery in Cuba. Permit me, by way of exordium, a few words on our ideas and on our Tribune. The title of this exordium will be

THE CUBAN TRIBUNE.

The ideas to which I am about to give expression, are based upon my convictions, and I would desire to see them instilled into the soul of every man. I address you with my heart on my lips, because I go to treat of the rights of the human race. I entertain no fear ; I respect every man's opinion ; and I consider myself as fulfilling a duty when I utter my own. It is in this way that I understand liberty. I see you before me, and not only you, but all Cubans, and universal humanity regarding and listening to me, attentive and silent. It is not pride, but rather sincerity that dictates to me the language ; and you should not blame me for it, as in doing so, you would be blaming yourselves. Yes, gentlemen, blaming yourselves ; for some of my ideas I have already indicated on this tribune, and their very indication has won for me your plaudits—plaudits which I bless, because they argue the identity of our sentiments. If there be any censure against me, it will be against you also; but I believe that you do not fear that censure, as I do not, since error alone can find fault with us for holding in our hearts the love of Cuba and the love of humanity identical. I said that I was about to speak of the Cuban tribune.

The Cuban tribune! This is it; a desk and a covering. Nothing more. Around are benches and arms which do not belong to us. Here there is nothing ours. Even the right to enter this hall costs us a sum; a petty sum which we poor exiles pay. But, gentlemen, our poverty is our greatness. The temple of Country is the temple of virtue, and in that temple, gold and decorations are dross and rags: in that temple nothing is esteemed save self-denial, patriotism and fraternity. Our poverty might appal us if it were the chastisement of our crimes; but the chastisement which iniquity applies to merit is merit's most resplendent aureöle. Our tyrants have been powerful enough to deprive us of our property, our family, and our firesides, but they could not take from us our patriotism, that moral gold whose degrees of fineness are purified by the fire of persecution. Our tyrants announce to the world "These filibusteros are some shirtless vagabonds whom we have driven from our colony." But the world regards us, for there are two things which the world cannot but regard: justice and misfortune. The world sees us proscribed, in exile; but it sees us, not uttering a useless and cowardly wailing, but serene, tranquil, panting to fly to Cuba to rescue our brothers from captivity; it sees us consecrated to the enlightenment of our minds; it sees us good men and honored; and it hears proclaimed from this tribunal the pure sentiment of our hearts. The merit of a tribune consists in the principles which are uttered from it; in the ideas of progress which irradiate from it; and in the political and moral doctrines which it enounces in defending the rights of man. That the world beholds in us, and its terrible malediction falls upon our tyrants.

Heretofore Cuba has not had a tribune. Here it is; poor, isolated, set in a foreign soil; and its first accents are not those of hate nor vengeance. No, the Cuban tribune causes to be heard the voice of truth, for that is the voice of history and of science; causes to be heard the voice of Justice, for that is the voice which sustains the rights of the peoples; and causes to be heard the voice of liberty, for that is the voice which determines the statutes of the human race.

Our tribune is poor; it is born humble and undraped; but its future is immense. Translated soon to our own soil, it will be occupied by Cubans who may enlighten the world with their eloquence. Liberty gives birth to Demosthenes and Ciceros. Our tribune is poor; but the Redeemer of the world was born in a manger. We ourselves are also poor; but in the temple of liberty there are no distinct seats for the poor and the rich, as in the temple of immortality there is no difference of place for the prosperous and the unfortunate. In that holy temple George Washington is as great, exercising the Presidency of the United States, as Narciso Lopez dying on the scaffold for the freedom of Cuba.

SLAVERY IS ANTAGONISTIC TO WEALTH.

There are three things that are inseparable: wealth, morality, and humanity. Some people believe that slavery, supposing it to be morally right, contributes to the production of wealth; a most fatal error, since political economy would not be a true science if it were not based on morality.

Let us seek in this science and in Christianity, the first argument to combat slavery. Morality is the science of what is just and unjust. Every man is called just or virtuous who is good, humane and a civilizer; and everything which is just is called good, because it produces inestimable benefits to the individual and to Society. Christianity is based on morality and virtue, and all its doctrines proclaim the fraternity of men. Paganism was contrary to morality, to virtue, and did not comprehend the meaning of human brotherhood. The greatness of the pagan peoples was a false greatness. Where temples were raised to lewd and vengeful qualities, where labor was ignominious, and where man was not the brother of man, there could not be greatness, because there could not be virtue. There existed not there, modest love, probity, conjugal fidelity, nor any of the Christian virtues. Therefore those peoples fell into decay.

Jesus Christ taught all the principles which constitute true morality, principles which serve as the foundation of his divine religion, and which have brought to the people wealth, science, progress and prosperity. Wealth is not merely material; it is likewise intellectual and moral; and material wealth cannot even exist without creating the other two. Therefore, slavery is contrary to the bases of Christianity, whose great doctrines are "Love thy neighbor as thyself," and "Do unto others what you would have others do unto you."

The second argument against slavery is presented to us by history. When in Rome the proprietors of the soil cultivated the land with their own hands, they occupied themselves solely in the camp and in labor. When Cincinnatus was informed of his elevation to the Dictatorship he was ploughing his field; and, hastening to his spouse, he said to her, "I fear that my little farm must remain untilled this year." Rome was not, at that time, the mistress of the world; but her fields were in the most flourishing condition. When that same Rome entrusted agriculture to slaves, so that they might acquire wealth with blood, their fields were so neglected that the conquerors of the world suffered wretchedness and starvation. Rome saw herself compelled to import corn from Sicily, from Spain and from Egypt; and, to have an idea of her wretchedness, it is merely necessary to remember that the Europe of that day did not produce, in one year, even half of the fruits which any of its states produces at present.

Rome always maintained slavery, and in this we have the explanation how it was that the Teutonic races parcelled among themselves her provinces, as birds of prey divide a dead body. The European peoples abolished slavery, and the manumissions were followed by the discovery of the compass, the press, the perfection of agriculture, the commercial exchanges between nations, the devolpment of the arts, schools, political right, and all the elements of wealth.

The Romans, with slaves, suffered hunger, nakedness and the yoke of their rulers ; the peoples of Europe, without slaves, commenced the grand era of civilization and prosperity.

History always presents to us identical examples ; but let us examine the relative worth of labor, as in the hands of the slave and in those of the free man.

Slaves are destined to domestic service, and to branches of industry. With respect to domestic service, experience shows that two free men work more than eight slaves ; and with respect to industrial occupations that the difference is still greater.

Let us see then the relative cost of free hands and slave hands. The free workman requires, in exchange for his labor, maintenance for himself and his family. The master of the slave must needs idemnify himself for the capital which his slave cost him, for the interest of that capital, for the expense of maintaining and providing for him medical attendance; and for the wages of the overseer. The comparison should not be made from individual to individual, but from property to property, or from factory to factory, since we have already seen that domestic service, as well as manufactures, require more or less hands just as these are free or slave. Let us also recollect that the slave does not live so long as the free worker, and we may draw the deduction that the work of the slave costs more than the work of the free laborer. But, it will be said, "Why do so many people then make use of slaves?" The answer is simple—because where slavery exists, domestic service and agricultural and manufacturing employments are degraded and are abandoned by free laborers : and hence it is that masters and contractors have no other resource but to recur to slave labor, under the penalty of abandoning their fields or their undertakings.

But, let us see why the free laborer performs more, better, and cheaper work than the slave. The free laborer keeps in view his fortune, his family, his future : he studies, economises, undertakes, improves, invents, and overcomes all obstacles. The slave expects nothing from his toil ; for him there is no stimulus but the whip ; and he has not before him any scheme for his own and his sons' future. He is, consequently, idle, insensible ; his very intelligence is his worst enemy, since it only serves to point out his misfortune. He does not reason ; he is stupid ; he cannot know the uses of machinery, the markets, the division of labor, nor their immense influence on the destiny of the individual and of society. Labor, with recompense, is man's first treasure ; but without reward it is only martyrdom. The utility of the slave is negative ; he does not devote his mind to work, but to avoid work.

In slave States, not only is labor deprived of the advantage of having intelligent and skillful workers, but free men are required to watch and rule over the slaves, instead of improving the work. To these two grave evils must be added another no less fatal, that, namely, of accustoming all persons connected with slavery to unite the ideas of production and slavery, so that they aspire to become rich only by augmenting the number of their slaves. Ah! there are now existing in Cuba five hundred thousand intelligent beings, dead so far as labor is concerned. What should you be, oh Cuba, were it not for slaves!

In all societies men are divided into capitalists and workers. But the workers do not live by the benevolence of capitalists; they live by what is more worthy. This world is God's world, and it is wonderfully organized. If there were no servants and laborers, capitalists and skillful men could not devote themselves to undertakings and inventions, since they would not have time to execute any of the works which are performed by the former. Capitalists live by workmen, as much as workmen live by capitalists. Their mutual wants are the providential means which form the bonds of human society and all the sources of wealth.

Slavery breaks these bonds. In slave countries, whenever the capitalist requires hands he purchases men. The majority of his fellows are men without capital, but the capitalists disregard them, and hence it is that the majority of such persons are in want of food, because they are in want of work.

Among these persons without capital, stand in the first rank women, particularly those who have lost parents, husbands, brothers. In a free country, as in New York for instance, there are for these women, workshops, manufactures, and every sort of occupation. In a land of slaves, as in Cuba, there are no workshops, and poor women are in want of the necessaries of life, because they have no business to apply themselves to. Nothing, gentlemen, nothing remains to these women, not even the humble resource of domestic service, since if they entered into it they would be confounded with slaves.

What is true of women in this respect, is equally true of children. In free countries they have workshops, and establishments, and schools; they can live, receive education, and even assist their indigent mothers. These children, in slave countries, have no occupation, and, instead of assisting their mothers, they only double the bitterness of their grief. Ah! this is horrible, because it is the truth.

The condition of men without capital is not less unfortunate in countries of slavery. They cannot become laborers, because the fields are cultivated by slaves; and they cannot devote themselves to occupations or branches of industry, because there are no workshops nor manufactories; and because the arts will not flourish where they are degraded by slavery.

Without morality there is no prosperity; but let us see how it is that slavery, wherever it exists, destroys morality. Without the whip there would be no slaves, since, by a natural law, man aspires to break all the obstacles which do violence to his understanding, to his will, and to his liberty. Masters, therefore, must be harsh, unjust, and inhuman. But, these masters have children; and the virtues which should be engraven on their souls are love, justice, and beneficence, or, in a single word, humanity. Consequently, the course which these masters have to pursue in regard to their slaves in the presence of their children, is for such children a school destructive to these virtues. These children, when their mind is opened to reason, believe that the just is unjust; believe that prosperity co-exists with slavery; believe that the evil is good, and that the inhuman is humane.

In connection with slavery, virtue is no longer virtue. For a slave woman to marry a slave and to preserve her conjugal fidelity, is to condemn herself and her children to slavery; and for that slave woman to surrender herself to a libertine, is to aspire to her own freedom and to the freedom of her children. This truth is seen in every slave country, a sad truth which is confirmed by the extraordinary number of children born of slave women out of the bonds of matrimony. And these slave women, for whom virtue is not virtue, nurse their masters' children, and have a large share in the formation of their first ideas. How deplorable for children are these two schools! the conduct of their fathers as masters, and the example of the nurses who attend on them from their cradle.

Labor is the only producer of wealth; and that law is a law of love, since it is it which maintains and binds societies together. Slavery violates that divine law in three senses: First, it takes from the slave that which God gave him, the fruit of his labor. Second, it gives to masters the fruit of a labor not theirs, though God has has declared to man "in the sweat of thy brow shalt thou eat bread." Third, it corrupts the soul of society with the anti-Christian doctrine and example that there may be wealth without toil, and morality with slavery.

From the doctrines laid down, these propositions spring; slavery is contrary to the morality and to the religion of Christ; the peoples who maintained slavery have eventually become impoverished and perished; Europe owes its present greatness to the manumission of slaves; slaves work badly as domestics and as laborers; slavery breaks the bonds which in every society unite capitalists with workmen; the masters of slaves must be unjust, a thing which is demoralizing to their children; slave women disregard virtue, thereby corrupting childhood and society; slavery deprives agriculture and the arts of the fecund impulse of intelligence; slave peoples have been unable to resist when tyrants oppressed or invaded them; and political economy, in accord with morality, sees in slavery a violation of the law of God, and the worst enemy of prosperity.

REFUTATION OF ARGUMENTS IN SUPPORT OF SLAVERY.

The arguments that are alleged in favor of slavery are nothing more than simple sophistries against Christianity, against morality, and against political economy. Let us look at these arguments.

First. "The patriarchs held slaves ; therefore slavery is good." The sacred Scriptures contain two distinct portions, one doctrinal, the other historical. The fact that the patriarchs held slaves belongs to the historical portion ; but this does not sanction, merely narrates ancient events, be they good or evil ; whilst the doctrinal portion of the Scriptures condemns all the errors on which the slavery of man is based. Besides, the word slavery or servitude has had distinct significations. The patriarchs did not mark the brow of the slave with iron, nor his condition with ignominy. Jacob became a servant that he might win the hand of Rachel. Joseph was a slave, and yet was the adviser of Pharaoh. At that time the world was not illumined with the light of the Gospel; and nevertheless the slavery of to-day is more horrible than it was in the early ages, and even among the enemies of the conquered people.

Second, " Slavery is a very delicate subject, and so to discuss it may produce enormous evils." I look upon it in this other light, " Slavery is a very delicate subject, and so not to discuss it may produce enormous evils." For these thirty years I have been accustomed to hear that it is not yet the proper time to discuss slavery. How is the time designated ? For me, it is always time to impugn whatever is evil, whatever is immoral, whatever outrages humanity, and whatever may inflict on Cuba great injuries. Man is distinguished from the brute by his intelligence, and the soul of intelligence is discussion. To combat slavery is to second the will of God.

Third. "To speak of emancipation, is to allow the slaves to learn that their freedom is pleaded for, which might impel them to declare it themselves." Even admitting that they might comprehend our desire, so long as that desire is good, moral and Christian, I can only deduce from it that it would attract to us their gratitude, their co-operation, and their enthusiasm for our own liberty.

Fourth. " Cuba, with slaves, has prospered much." Cuba has no workshops, maaufactories, schools, occupations for indigent women and children ; it has no roads, canals, immigration ; it has no sovereignty ; it has no laws ; it has not even peace for the repose of its children. That is not prosperity, and if it be so designated I do not desire it for my country. It is true that the agriculture of Cuba has progressed considerably in half a century ; but the progress which that agriculture has made with slaves is in proportion to what it would have made without them, as one to a thousand. God has not condemned any country to hold slaves, and least of all Cuba, where labor obtains an hundredfold reward, and whose virgin lands, refreshed with the breezes of the temperate zone of the north, allure her sons with all the tropical products. Texas, in a few years, has increased her population tenfold ; and California has increased hers with greater rapidity. Cuba, without slaves and with good laws, might have millions of souls.

Fifth. " In all Republics, including that of the United States, there have been slaves." To think thus, is to be ignorant of human progress. Not only Republics, but all countries, have had idolatry, theocracy, tyranny, the rack, dislike to labor, a restrictive system, and even human victims; and these institutions have fallen as slavery shall fall, or rather as it is falling. Feudal Europe had slaves; so had the Spanish American republics. Tunis had them; and the English and French colonies had them; they have them no longer. When science proclaims an idea which is good, civilizing and moral, the people are not slow to adopt it; and if they do not attempt it at the instant, it is because despots prohibit it, or because the people are meditating upon it. But I will limit myself to the existence of slaves in the United States. The errors of society are the condition of progress. With the compass, by which the immense progresses of the United States are measured, with that compass are measured, also, the immense errors which her laws have corrected; and those errors are nothing more than the gloomy legacy of the old British legislation. The United States, from the time of her independence, comprehended how fatal a thing slavery is. Mistress of her own destiny, her first step was its destruction.

With the independence of the United States the African trade ceased; in the northern States slavery was abolished; the foundation of Liberia—an idea the most honorable to civilization—is a new bulwark against slavery in this country; and California has already emancipated the slaves which were within her borders. Here are arguments which are facts, and which afford confirmation that the United States are endeavoring to extinguish slavery.

Sixth. "To speak against slavery is to alienate the southern States of the American Union from the cause of Cuba." If to combat slavery were to alienate the South from our cause, it would, for the same reason, attract the North to its support; consequently the loss would be compensated, and the duty of opposing slavery would not have even the shadow of objection. But the southern States of America, as well as the the northern States, are interested in behalf of Cuba; not because she may or may not have slaves, but that they may establish in Cuba new markets, new branches of business, new sources of wealth, and that they may export from the mouth of the Mississippi, and from other centres of trade, their products into the adjacent points of Cuba. Besides, what injury would the Southern States sustain by our emancipating our slaves? California has liberated hers, and the same interest in her continues to inspire them; the Northern States emancipated theirs also, and their interest in them has not altered. The same thing would take place with respect to Cuba, who, by the Federal Constitution of the United States would be always authorized to keep or to manumit her slaves according as it served her uses and pleasure.

Seventh. "Many Cubans will regard independence as an evil, if it involve the liberation of the slaves, and, far from coöperating in it, will remain indifferent, or will support the Spanish Government." I do not believe thus of my countrymen; I consider them as being more intelligent, more sensible, and possessing more patriotism and more humanity. I believe that the Cubans thoroughly comprehend that labor depends on intelligence, that our want of workshops and our industrial backwardness proceed solely from slavery ; I believe that they are interested in the condition of our poor women, that they are not ignorant that slavery is demoralizing, and that they know that with slavery there is no security for their wealth, nor future for their children. If the Cubans now make use of slave labor, it is because the Spanish Government is opposed to the existence of other labor. Don Domingo Goicouria, and other good Cubans, have solicited permission to introduce white laborers, and have presented projects and means for the carrying out of their idea, and the Spanish Government has always repulsed them, that it might continue the African slave trade. But the Cubans would prefer free laborers, because they are not insensate, and because they understand the civilization of the nineteenth century, a civilization which point the harmonies existing between wealth, intelligence, and the doctrines of morality. To unite, therefore, the cause of humanity to that of the independence of Cuba is not to drive from it our brothers ; it is, on the contrary to enlist them under its banner.

Eighth. " To emancipate the Cuban slaves, is to place the blacks on an equal footing in every respect with the white, to which even the bitterest abolitionists are opposed." This sophism is even ridiculous. In the northern States there are great numbers of free negroes, and they have schools, churches, societies of various kinds, and even military companies, without there being that identification which it is pretended to dread. In the southern States, as well as in Cuba, there are very many free negroes, and there does not exist any such mixture with the whites. Laws are one thing, and customs another. To plead that there be no slaves in a country is not to plead for the mixture of two different races. If slavery were abolished in Cuba, the slaves of to-day would be elevated to the rank which free negroes enjoy, to their own benefit and ours. That will be always the result of everything which is good, moral, humane, and Christian.

Ninth. " To emancipate the negroes is to give them an opportunity of becoming enlightened and of destroying us." The history of slaves is the history of conspirators, of the enemies of labor, of political revolts, and of the demoralization and extermination of peoples ; to give to the slaves liberty, property, intelligence, family interests, and a future, is to interest them in the peace, the order, the labor, the morality and the well-being of societies. History teaches that, our eyes see that, and it is taught to us by morality, political economy, Christianity, and even by common sense, Slavery is contrary to nature, and to abolish that which is contrary to nature is not to injure but to save societies.

MEANS OF ABOLISHING SLAVERY IN CUBA.

If I might only obey the desires of my soul, the law of manumission for the slaves of Cuba would be very simple : " *All the slaves of Cuba are declared free.*" These should be the words of the law which I should propose ; but slavery is such a horrible thing that once established, it is very difficult to eradicate it ; a truth which is proved to us by the fifty years' discussion in the British Parliament, and by the existence of slaves in the Southern States of the American Union.

Cuba holds five hundred thousand slaves, and we have already stated that every slave sees in labor the instrument of his misfortune, that his understanding is vitiated, and that he has very incorrect ideas of what is just and moral, and of religion. Our slaves, particularly those of the country, have no foresight ; therefore, to emancipate them suddenly would be to ruin our agriculture, our arts ; it would be to leave ourselves without domestics ; it would be to rob their masters of the capital represented by those slaves whom they acquired legitimately ; and it would be to subject ourselves to all the excesses to which they might be impelled by ignorance, hunger, and the dislike to toil. But, everything is reconciled by intelligence. When we believe it impossible to do anything that is good, that is moral, that is Christian, we should not say *we cannot*, but *we know not how*.

To reconcile the liberation of our slaves with the conservation of our wealth and safety, I will indicate the means which I believe most opportune and most convenient for all the sons of Cuba. These means would free our native land from the germ of death which it contains for labor, for its morality, for its political and economical condition, for its present state, and for its future destiny.

In my opinion, the liberation of our slaves, that is to say, the price of their liberty, should fall upon all the inhabitants of Cuba, including themselves ; but I do not believe that possible, and I only desire that we should approach to what may facilitate that just division.

I wish, first, to estimate what the masters of slaves should gain, to compare it afterwards with what they should lose ; and, at present, I allude only to material gains and losses, since the moral benefit which the abolition of slavery would produce to all, is inestimable.

I am not sufficiently vain to believe that the means which I am about to indicate are capable of no improvement ; nothing is further from my ideas. And would that other minds occupying themselves with a subject so vital for Cuba and for humanity, may present other means more easy, prompt, just, and beneficent; I should be the first to sustain them. I do not know why it is that the minds of Cuba do not deliberate on this important subject ; even though they should not do it for the sake of humanity, they ought to be occupied with it; since, if we do not work for the gradual emancipation of our slaves, we run the risk of its being brought about suddenly, and of bringing in its train unspeakable misfortunes. This ill may come upon us from the English Government, from the Spanish, from the Haïtien, and even through the agency of our slaves themselves. None but foolish minds believe that the slaves of to-morrow will be the slaves of to-day, as if the same rule which applies to individual life did not also apply to social life.

But, let us see the measures which I propose.

First. "Cuba shall be free and independent." I understand by "independent," that she will be radically and for ever separated from the Spanish Government. I am no concessionist. What could that government do for Cuba, which has produced naught but misfortunes to the whole Continent of America, and to Spain herself? That government sacrificed our Indians, separated us first from the world, then inundated us with African slaves, and to-day dictates for us laws which are the dishonor of civilization and the scandal of Christianity. In Cuba there will be slaves so long as there is a Spanish Government; and I abhor that government, because I desire the benefits of liberty for the inhabitants of Cuba—be they Creoles or Peninsulars—and for all men.

Second. "Cuba shall be Republican." I understand by "republican," that she have a popular government, with liberty of the press, of commerce, and of worship; that she foster industry and education, and that she assure her well-being and safety by becoming allied or annexed to the United States. With these institutions, Cuba would be filled with toilers, and her industries would be fecund, because they would be intelligent. To-day, Cubans cannot carry anything from one point to another, not even their own persons, without being detained by the petty officers of the law. The birds in the air, the fish in the sea, and the wild beasts in the forests, have more freedom than we have. But, I am mistaken: in Cuba there is no wild beast other than the Spanish Government—a wild beast which has engendered a two-headed monster, domestic slavery and political slavery.

Third. "Cessation of the African Slave trade." That trade will continue in Cuba whilst the Spanish government rules there, since it serves its policy and its treasury. In Cuba the trade will cease with the attainment of her independence, as took place in the United States, where Africans ceased to be brought, and where the free laborers who emigrated thither, were counted by hundreds of thousands.

Fourth. "To abolish; 1st, all the taxes paid by rural properties; 2d, the customs from lands and slaves; 3d, every duty on the exportation of the products of the soil; and 4th, every duty on the importation of utensils and machines for agriculture, and on the wearing apparel and food for slaves. A portion of the revenues of the country shall be also devoted to the improvement of communications by land and water." The disposition in this article will indemnify masters for the prejudice which they may sustain by the two following.

Fifth. "The maximum price of a slave shall be $700 up to the year 1860. $600 thence till the year 1870, and $100 less for each decade until the complete extinction of slavery." This law would be very important, since without it we would have to contend with the inconveniences of a sudden manumission, or with those of perpetuating slavery in Cuba. Thus, therefore, to assure its benefits, this rule should form part of the political constitution of Cuba, and every pretension directed in opposition to it should be held as an attempt against that constitution. But let us see the last article before analyzing the present.

Sixth. "Liberty to the children of our slave women who may be born in future, then there can be no more slaves born in Cuba." This humane law would be for slave fathers the greatest of benefits ; and that new generation would not abhor labor, since it would see in industry its subsistence, its well-being, and its future. These children would form a new tie between the master and his slaves. The master in treating them well would have the best means of stimulating their parents to work ; and the latter in their turn would endeavor to merit this kindness towards their children by persevering in work. Some say that the master would disregard these children to the point that they would perish for want of care ; but I believe that there is more goodness in our breasts than those who speak so suppose.

Humanity is a law of God, and the laws of God always stand as tribunals in every human conscience. I believe, apart from our philanthropy, that the loss which would accrue to masters from the maintenance of these creatures and from the cares which their mothers have to bestow on them, is insignificant compared to the utility which they would derive from the good service of their parents, for whom there would be a future inasmuch as the future of their children would be theirs.

The price of $700 per slave, in no respect prejudices owners, since the average value of a slave in Cuba is from $500 to $600. Supposing that the law should be enacted in the year 1854, it would follow that up to the year 1869, a slave would be worth $600; that is to say, that the master would have enjoyed him for the space of fifteen years, without a diminution of his value ; in twenty-five years after the passage of the law, the slave would be worth $500. It is certain that the law being enacted, the master would have to maintain the children of slaves born in future, and that after the lapse of fifteen years, he would lose $100 every ten years in the value of a slave : but the benefit which the fourth article produces to him, is much greater than these two evils ; much greater, because it leaves him more money than the price of the slave is diminished ; and much greater, because the benefit of that article is permanent, whilst the evil of the emancipation is temporal.

Another great benefit in the plan which I propose is, that the masters have time to set about replacing the slaves with free men ; reckoning among these latter the children of the slaves, who will see in labor the foundation of their future, and not the worst of their enemies.

I do not forget that it is not only the owners of plantations who have slaves, and that the proposed emancipation would also fall upon all slave owners ; but the relief from the duties of exportation and the other administrative reforms before indicated, will leave in their hands, and permanently, a greater sum than what they lose. These masters, besides, enjoy for fifteen years the labor of their slaves, without any abatement of their price, an abatement which will not begin to take place until the benefits enjoyed are received for some years, and until the immigration of free hands lessens the wages of workmen and of domestic servants.

It will appear to some that the preceding plan embraces a very long period; and to others a very short one. I will reply to the first, that the life of societies is not measured with the same compass as that of individuals; that to embrace too much is frequently not to attain anything; and that in the country of Washington, there would not to-day be a slave, if their legislators had adopted the plan which we are discussing. I believe that the American people in establishing their independence, would not have hesitated in adopting such a plan; and yet now, perhaps, it would meet some difficulties. All things have more or less a time and a season, and that which I have just shown in respect to the United States is applicable to Cuba. If the day of emancipation be somewhat distant, no injury will accrue to the holders of slaves, and the lovers of Cuba and of humanity will at least die with the pleasure of contemplating a future not very far removed in which there shall not be in our country any but freemen.

Those who consider the time proposed too short, I would only ask to study history, the science of economy, and the human heart; and if these three books, which do not lie, are not sufficient to convince them, I would advise them to examine the statistics of Cuba and of the neighboring islands, and the principles of Christianity, either in a religious or scientific sense; they would plead then for the brevity of the time.

It is more than time to come to a conclusion. To liberate our slaves is to fulfil the law of God; and to fulfil the law of God does not offer those inconveniences which error exaggerates. Sons of Cuba, I appeal to you and to posterity. If we emancipate our slaves, we will be astonished at our physical and moral progress; if we do not emancipate them, we will be doubly parricides, because we will deprive our children of physical wealth and moral wealth. Since we are adopting the immense benefits of civilization, let us be consistent and adopt also the petty sacrifices which it requires from us and for our advancement. That civilization, Jesus Christ, history, and our conscience cry to us against slavery. Almost all countries have had slavery, and have got rid of it. Always by the side of slavery are seen hunger, vices, and serfdom; while the Christian principle of the fraternity of men is ever accompanied by well-being, virtue, peace and happiness. Let us not forget it; there is no prosperity without industry; there is no industry without intelligence; there is no intelligence without virtue; there is no virtue without religion; and there is no religion where there is slavery. The sacrifices which the manumission of our slaves may cost us are but temporary; the benefits will be eternal, as the father of humanity is eternal. These sacrifices will be the best offering to our sons, to our country, and to God. All the intellects of Cuba are opposed to slavery, and more than one illustrious Cuban has liberated his slaves. In that number figures one of our heroes, Don Joaquin Aguëro.

In my humble opinion, not to unite the emancipation of our slaves to the independence of Cuba—and in such a manner as not to admit doubts and procrastinations—is to inoculate in our political regeneration a fatal germ of unlimited misfortunes. I see the fall of Greece, Rome, and Carthage, because they had slavery. I see the Spanish-American Republics stumbling in the path of liberty; and I see in them merely the footsteps of slavery. I see the aborigines of Cuba disappear, and I see only the effect of slavery: and I see sanguinary wars between the Turks and Christians, solely on account of slavery. I see in Africa a market of human flesh, sustained by slavery. I see despots on the earth, because their power is based on slavery; and I see our heroes perish on scaffolds, because slavery reigns in Cuba. I see, in fine, the misfortune of our land, and of the whole earth, still growing from slavery. I have but one voice and one heart, and my voice and my heart are for Cuba and for humanity, because God and nature proclaim the liberty of the human race.

www.ingramcontent.com/pod-product-compliance
Lightning Source LLC
LaVergne TN
LVHW020639110826
845149LV00004B/1286

9781418190415